This is Definitely NOT Y

Foo

By N

Welcome to *This is Definitely NOT your Bog-Standard Quiz Book: Food & Drink*.

Firstly this book is principally aimed at Brits at home and ex-pats and here is what you'll find inside ...

The questions have been researched and collected by me over a period of over 30 years and the book contains questions that you will never before have seen in any other quiz book.

There are 500 questions split into 50 quizzes of 10 questions each. Usefully there are 500 answers too which are on the page immediately following each quiz. They are randomly selected and they are not collected into themed sections.

There are some easy ones. There are some hard ones. There are some that fall anywhere in between.

While the overall theme of the book is food and drink you will find questions on ... foods, both British and foreign. Drinks, both alcoholic and non. Restaurants. Chefs. Sweets. Television programmes and adverts. Films. Music. Literature. Slogans. Art. And much more.

All questions and answers are correct as at August 2017, the date of publication. E&OE

I hope you enjoy it. Other titles by me will be available in the future or if not published already.

QUIZ 1

1 In a Punch & Judy show when Joey the Clown announces that it's dinner time what food is produced, whereupon the crocodile also appears?

2 A polar bear named Peppy is the mascot of which brand of mint confection?

3 In which country might you eat poffertjes, stroopwafel, oliebollen, ontbijtkoek, bitterballen and snert?

4 What food is nicknamed a Glasgow salad?

5 Who won the 6th series of *The Great British Bake-Off* and has gone on to present TV programmes, write newspaper and magazine columns and publish a children's book called *Bake Me a Story*?

6 What is the name of the tall white, pleated, starched hat worn by some chefs?

7 As in the TV adverts, which food retailer "gets a 10 from Len"? (Len Goodman)

8 Which film star opened Langan's Brasserie with Peter Langan in London in 1976?

9 What is the name of Munich's world famous annual beer festival which is also known locally as Wiesn?

10 Which popular brand of tea is made by Taylor's of Harrogate?

ANSWERS 1

1 SAUSAGES
2 FOX'S GLACIER MINTS
3 THE NETHERLANDS
4 CHIPS
5 NADIYA HUSSEIN
6 TOQUE (TOQUE BLANCHE)
7 FARMFOODS
8 MICHAEL CAINE
9 OKTOBERFEST
10 YORKSHIRE TEA

QUIZ 2

1 The Carron Fish Bar in Stonehaven, Aberdeenshire attracts tourists from all over the world as it claims to be "The Birthplace of the Deep-Fried ..." what?

2 In a *Doctor Who* episode called 'The Eleventh Hour' the Doctor (Matt Smith) ate what with his fish fingers?

3 What colour is Guinness?

4 In February 2017 Wayne Shaw resigned as a goalkeeper with Sutton United after a stunt in which he was seen, as the reserve keeper on the bench, eating what during an FA Cup match with Arsenal?

5 Which Cumbrian town is noted for its mint cake?

6 Seed Sensations is a bread brand of which company that is jointly owned by The Gores Group and Premier Foods?

7 Which 1997 film's working title was *Eggs, Beans & Chippendales*?

8 Which snack food brand's mascot is Mr. Peanut?

9 Who painted the 1885 painting *The Potato Eaters*?

10 Point 8 of which political party's 2016 Manicfesto (sic) for the Welsh Assembly elections was the proposal to legalise broccoli?

ANSWERS 2

1 MARS BAR
2 CUSTARD
3 RUBY RED (* See note below)
4 A PIE
5 KENDAL
6 HOVIS
7 THE FULL MONTY
8 PLANTERS
9 VINCENT VAN GOGH
10 OFFICIAL MONSTER RAVING LOONY PARTY

* (From the Guinness website – "Guinness beer is not actually black but rather dark ruby red because of the way the ingredients are prepared. Some malted barley is roasted, in a similar way to coffee beans, which is what gives Guinness its distinctive colour.")

QUIZ 3

1 What is said to be the most important meal of the day?

2 What shape is the jam hole in a Burton's Jammie Dodger?

3 Madame Cholet is which characters' cook?

4 What word can come before pie, egg, pancake and broth?

5 Which supermarket company began life as a butter and egg merchant in Bradford in 1899?

6 In which TV series was Artie Bucco Jr. the co-owner and head chef of the Nuovo Vesuvio restaurant?

7 What name is given to a 9 gallon beer barrel?

8 Which suet-based pudding is nicknamed Dead Man's Arm or Dead Man's Leg?

9 Which port has been dubbed "Britain's fish-processing capital"?

10 In American diner slang how does someone want their eggs cooked if the cook is told to "Wreck a pair"?

ANSWERS 3

1 BREAKFAST
2 HEART
3 THE WOMBLES
4 SCOTCH
5 MORRISONS
6 THE SOPRANOS
7 FIRKIN
8 ROLY-POLY
9 GRIMSBY
10 SCRAMBLED

QUIZ 4

1 Which coffee house chain was named after the first mate of the *Pequod* whaling ship in the story of *Moby-Dick*?

2 We were once informed in the adverts that which beer was "reassuringly expensive"?

3 Which country has the most restaurants with at least one Michelin star? (Exactly 600 in 2016 guide)

4 What is the name of the Hawaiian-themed burger chain in the Quentin Tarantino films *Pulp Fiction* and *Reservoir Dogs*?

5 In Italy which cheese is known as The King of Cheeses?

6 In British army slang what are 'canteen medals'?

7 What would you use a swizzle stick for?

8 What name is given to a block of chocolate consisting of strawberry, vanilla and chocolate flavours?

9 In which mines in Knotty Ash do the Diddy Men work?

10 Which company has been serving Happy Meals since 1979?

ANSWERS 4

1 STARBUCKS
2 STELLA ARTOIS
3 FRANCE
4 BIG KAHUNA BURGER
5 PARMIGGIANO-REGGIANO (PARMESAN)
6 FOOD STAINS ON CLOTHES
7 STIRRING A COCKTAIL
8 NEAPOLITAN
9 JAM BUTTY MINES
10 McDONALD'S

QUIZ 5

1 With a similar logo, which brand of potato crisps are sold in some other countries under the Lay's name?

2 At which football stadium is the Highbury Restaurant?

3 In 2016 scientists conducted a study of Britain's best dunking biscuits with the best being able to survive 14 dunks in hot tea or coffee. So which biscuit came out as the most durable (not favourite but durable)? (The study was conducted for McVitie's)

4 Which instant hot snack food brand is one of the nicknames of Chinese snooker player Ding Junhui?

5 According to the National Federation of Fish Fryers which variety is regarded as the best potato for chips?

6 What did Alice eat in Wonderland to make her grow tall?

7 Who painted *Le déjeuner sur l'herbe* (The luncheon on the grass) in 1863?

8 Which BBC radio and TV presenter owns the Mulberry Inn, in Chiddingfold, Surrey where every Friday is TFI Pie Day?

9 In 2010 and 2011 *Rock & Chips* was a 3-part prequel to which long-running TV sitcom?

10 Magners is a brand of what drink?

ANSWERS 5

1 WALKER'S
2 THE EMIRATES STADIUM (Arsenal)
3 RICH TEA
4 POT NOODLE
5 MARIS PIPER
6 CAKE
7 ÉDOUARD MANET
8 CHRIS EVANS
9 ONLY FOOLS AND HORSES
10 CIDER

QUIZ 6

1 What does the 55 mean in the Britvic 55 brand?

2 According to Cadbury, the filling in which of their products is called goo?

3 De Koninck's is a major brewery in which country?

4 What names does celebrity chef Ainsley Harriott call his salt and pepper mills?

5 In which 1980 Martin Scorcese boxing film does an over-cooked steak ignite the wrath of Robert De Niro?

6 In which Steven Sondheim musical is the song *The Worst Pies in London*?

7 According to the company themselves there are how many teaspoons of sugar in one 330ml can of regular Coca-Cola?

8 Who wrote the 2011 book *My Kitchen Table: 100 Cakes and Bakes*?

9 In the 1960s which brand name condiment was dubbed "Wilson's gravy"? (For former Prime Minister Harold Wilson)

10 Who is the mascot of Bassett's sweets?

ANSWERS 6

1 55% PURE JUICE (The label now states that it's actually 58%)
2 CRÈME EGGS
3 BELGIUM
4 SUZIE & PERCY
5 RAGING BULL
6 SWEENEY TODD: THE DEMON BARBER OF FLEET STREET
7 7
8 MARY BERRY
9 HP SAUCE
10 BERTIE BASSETT

QUIZ 7

1 The opening lyrics of Larry Williams' 1958 rock'n'roll song *Bony Moronie* are: "I got a girl named Bony Moronie, she's as skinny as a ..." what?

2 How do Heinz spell the word 'beans'?

3 In France what is the filling in 'un sandwich Belge' (a Belgian sandwich)?

4 According to the Office for National Statistics what was the average price of a pint of lager in 1991?

5 Which brand of cider got its name from the nickname of Cambro-Norman knight Richard de Clare, later the Earl of Pembroke?

6 As in the Charles Dickens novel Oliver Twist said: "Please sir, I want some more." Of what food did he want more?

7 Under normal playing conditions how long is the lunch break in a cricket test match?

8 The name of which alcoholic drink brand translates into English as 'hunting master'?

9 What variety of apple is the logo of The Beatles Apple record label?

10 What is a Norfolk Knob?

ANSWERS 7

1 STICK OF MACARONI
2 BEANZ
3 CHIPS (POMMES FRITES)
4 £1·37
5 STRONGBOW
6 GRUEL
7 40 MINUTES
8 JAGERMEISTER
9 GRANNY SMITH
10 BISCUIT

QUIZ 8

1 What is Bart Simpson's "most hated of all loaves"?

2 Which cold Spanish soup's three main ingredients are tomato, cucumber and peppers?

3 In which town can you visit Bettys Café Tea Rooms at 1 Parliament Street?

4 Which Heinz product, sold in jars, is nicknamed Mad Dog Vomit or Baby Sick?

5 In which 2002 romcom film does Sandra Bullock, as Lucy Kelson, order Chinese takeaway over the phone usually stating that it's for one but, at the end of the film orders for two people?

6 Who opened his first fish and chip shop in 1928 in a wooden hut in White Cross, Guiseley in West Yorkshire?

7 What was advertised in a 1980s TV commercial which ended with one young football fan questioning "Accrington Stanley? Who are they?" and the other lad saying "Exactly!"?

8 What is an ice cream cone with a Flake called?

9 Which Cornish port is home to a number of eating establishments owned by Rick Stein such as The Seafood Restaurant and St. Petroc's Bistro and also shops and a cookery school?

10 What is the French name of the dish in which mussels are cooked in white wine?

ANSWERS 8

1 MEAT LOAF
2 GAZPACHO
3 HARROGATE
4 SANDWICH SPREAD
5 TWO WEEKS NOTICE
6 HARRY RAMSDEN
7 MILK
8 99
9 PADSTOW
10 MOULES MARINIÈRE

QUIZ 9

1 According to the lyrics of the song what does Molly Malone sell from her wheelbarrow?

2 Lasagne was created by Luigi Lasagne in the 15th century: true or false?

3 For the coronation banquet of which monarch was the dish Coronation Chicken created by Constance Spry and Elizabeth Hume?

4 According to the British Egg Information Service approximately one in every thousand hens' eggs is what?

5 Which comedian wears a belt with a buckle that spells the word 'BEER'?

6 In France what simple dish is 'fèves au lard sur du pain grillé'?

7 What is the name of the place on board a boat where food is prepared and cooked?

8 Which Carry On film ended in a massive food fight and caption "And so they were all married and fought happily ever after"?

9 What has been advertised with the slogan "Get that Friday feeling"?

10 Aisukurimu (アイスクリム) is the Japanese word for what food?

ANSWERS 9

1 COCKLES AND MUSSELS
2 FALSE
3 ELIZABETH II
4 A DOUBLE YOLK EGG
5 AL MURRAY / THE PUB LANDLORD
6 BEANS ON TOAST
7 GALLEY
8 CARRY ON LOVING
9 CRUNCHIE
10 ICE CREAM

QUIZ 10

1 Schwarzwälder Kirschtorte is the German name for which cake?

2 Which strong Carlsberg beer was created in 1950 in honour of Winston Churchill?

3 Which company owns the Brewers Fayre and Beefeater pub restaurants?

4 What is the dipper in a Barratt's Sherbet Fountain?

5 Which famous mustard manufacturing company was established in 1814 in Norwich?

6 Which character in a 1962 Pat Boone hit single says: "Hey Rosita, I have to go shopping downtown for my mother. She needs some tortillas and chilli peppers"?

7 In *Quality Street* chocolates what colour wrapper and shape is the hazelnut noisette?

8 Which fictional British archaeologist and treasure hunter's favourite meal is beans on toast?

9 What brand name product's slogan is "Aah!" as appears on the packaging?

10 Which chocolate bar was created in 1930 and named after one of the Mars family's horses?

ANSWERS 10

1 BLACK FOREST CAKE / GATEAU
2 SPECIAL BREW
3 WHITBREAD
4 LIQUORICE STICK
5 COLMAN'S
6 SPEEDY GONZALES
7 GREEN TRIANGLE
8 LARA CROFT
9 BISTO
10 SNICKERS

QUIZ 11

1 Paul Newman ate 50 of what in the film *Cool Hand Luke*?

2 Bottles of which French wine brand are easily identifiable by their unique wonky shape?

3 In 1967 Jim Delligatti, who died on 28 November 2016, created what item on a McDonald's restaurant menu?

4 How many segments are there in a Terry's Chocolate Orange?

5 What is the UK's best-selling popcorn brand?

6 Which group had a Top 10 hit in 1989 with the song *Chocolate Box*?

7 What are the two rationed staple foods that contestants get to eat daily in *I'm A Celebrity … Get Me Out of Here*?

8 Which company operates Europe's largest food processing factory at Kitt Green, Wigan?

9 What is the name of the company set up by Prince Charles in 1990 and whose first product was an oaten biscuit?

10 In 2005 which Bernard Matthews product became a much discussed subject after Jamie Oliver got it removed from school lunch menus?

ANSWERS 11

1 BOILED EGGS
2 J.P. CHENET
3 BIG MAC
4 20
5 BUTTERKIST
6 BROS
7 RICE & BEANS
8 HEINZ
9 DUCHY ORIGINALS (Now Waitrose Duchy Organic)
10 TURKEY TWIZZLERS

QUIZ 12

1 Which Crosse & Blackwell pickle is named after a village in Staffordshire?

2 What type of porridge is one of the signature dishes of Heston Blumenthal?

3 What do the letters of the British restaurant chain GBK stand for?

4 What is the Official Pie of the state of Vermont in the USA?

5 Whose BBC Radio 6 Music show (two joint presenters) is described in a jingle recorded by Kirsty Young as "Fish and chips for the ears"?

6 Which singer wanted to have *Dinner With Gershwin* – the title of a hit single for her in 1987?

7 What type of alcoholic drinks are Martini Bianco, Cinzano Bianco and Noilly Prat?

8 Which Thai beer brand were the main sponsors of Everton football club from 2004 to 2017?

9 Who hosts a banquet every November at the Mansion House in London at which the Prime Minister gives a keynote speech?

10 Reputedly introduced by Butlins in 2003 what number in bingo lingo is called as 'Chicken Vindaloo'?

ANSWERS 12

1 BRANSTON
2 SNAIL
3 GOURMET BURGER KITCHEN
4 APPLE PIE
5 MARK RADCLIFFE & STUART MACONIE
6 DONNA SUMMER
7 VERMOUTH
8 CHANG
9 LORD MAYOR OF LONDON
10 52

QUIZ 13

1 In which Lerner & Loewe musical is the song *Hand Me Down That Can O' Beans*?

2 During the period of Ramadan in Islam bottles of which purple-coloured soft drink, first made in Manchester in 1908, sees a huge spike in sales in the Gulf States as it is drunk with meals to break the daily fast?

3 Which apple variety was named after the orchard near Motueka in New Zealand where it was first grown commercially?

4 In the TV soap *Emmerdale* who is the chef (and barman) at Woolpack pub?

5 What colour is the packaging of a lamb OXO stock cube?

6 Of what type of meat is there a cut called scrag end?

7 A computer-generated image of which film star sitting on a bus, and then in a car, is in a TV advert for Galaxy chocolate accompanied by her singing *Moon River*

8 Who levitated and then sent Aunt Petunia's Violet Pudding down on the head of Mrs. Mason in the film *Harry Potter and the Chamber of Secrets*?

9 What does it mean if a wine should be served 'chambré'?

10 What is mixed with Tia Maria to make a Tia Moo Moo cocktail?

ANSWERS 13

1 PAINT YOUR WAGON
2 VIMTO
3 BRAEBURN
4 MARLON DINGLE
5 PURPLE
6 LAMB or MUTTON
7 AUDREY HEPBURN
8 DOBBY
9 ROOM TEMPRATURE
10 MILK

QUIZ 14

1 At which fast food chain can you have a Zinger Burger, Daddy Burger or a Fillet Tower Burger?

2 What was the name of the Cadbury chocolate bar launched in 1970, no longer made for UK market, that contained rum-flavoured raisins?

3 On a German dining table what are 'ein messer und ein gabel'?

4 Which actor, born in 1962 and brought up in a children's home, owns the Plume of Feathers pub and restaurant in Barlaston in Staffordshire?

5 Starmix, Super Mix, Tangfastics, Goldbears, Chamallows and Strawbs are brands of which German confectionery company?

6 In the film *Monty Python's Meaning of Life* what food proved to be too much for the obese, gluttonous diner Mr. Creosote causing him to explode?

7 Where does Paddington bear keep his 'emergency' marmalade sandwich?

8 Which blue humanoid characters are 3 apples tall?

9 Which organisation has, since 1977, staged the annual Great British Beer Festival which since 1992 has been held either at Olympia or Earl's Court in London?

10 In cooking what French term is used for a dish that is encased in pastry?

ANSWERS 14

1 KFC
2 OLD JAMAICA
3 A KNIFE & FORK
4 NEIL MORRISSEY
5 HARIBO
6 A WAFER-THIN MINT
7 IN HIS HAT
8 SMURFS
9 CAMPAIGN FOR REAL ALE (CAMRA)
10 EN CROUTE

QUIZ 15

1 Which British celebrity chef has five eating establishments in Las Vegas, the latest of which was the Fish & Chips restaurant that opened at 3545 Las Vegas Boulevard in October 2016?

2 Which American city claims the invention of the deep-pan pizza at the Pizzeria Uno in 1943?

3 Which TV cook and writer's 2003 autobiography *Toast: The Story of a Boy's Hunger* was adapted for the 2010 BBC TV drama just called *Toast*?

4 *Chippy Tea* is the most well-known song of which comedy group from St. Helens?

5 Which darts commentator said: "The atmosphere is so tense if Elvis walked in with a portion of chips you could hear the vinegar sizzle on them."?

6 Which fish-canner was born in Linlithgow, Scotland in 1810 and started his canning operations in Oregon in 1868?

7 What type of food is a phall?

8 What sweets did Beatles fans used to throw at them when performing on stage during the height of Beatlemania?

9 In a 2007 interview actress Maria Schneider said that she did not use what foodstuff anymore since appearing with Marlon Brando in the film *Last Tango in Paris*?

10 Complete the old advertising slogan "Don't say brown, say …"?

ANSWERS 15

1 GORDON RAMSAY
2 CHICAGO
3 NIGEL SLATER
4 THE LANCASHIRE HOTPOTS
5 SID WADDELL
6 JOHN WEST
7 CURRY
8 JELLY BABIES
9 BUTTER
10 HOVIS

QUIZ 16

1 What is the name of the classic noodle-based street food of Thailand whose name means "fried Thai-style"?

2 In which series of novels and films might the characters eat Chocolate Frogs, Acid Pops, Cockroach Clusters and Cauldron Cakes?

3 Which American singer had a No.2 hit single in 2003 with the song *Milkshake* from her album *Tasty*?

4 What name is given to the style of serving food at a formal dinner where the waiter uses a fork and a spoon in one hand to serve the food to the diner's plate

5 Who wrote the 1999 novel *Chocolat* in which Vianne Rocher opens a chocolaterie?

6 What does Yogi Bear like to steal from visitors to Jellystone Park?

7 Which coffee was famously advertised in the 1980s and 1990s in an ongoing series of TV adverts featuring Sharon Maughan and Anthony Head in a slowly developing romance?

8 Which Stoke-on-Trent brewery produces the beers White Star, Captain Smith's, Lifeboat, First Class, Steerage and Iceberg?

9 What is the name of the kitchen gadget that can be used to turn courgettes, potatoes, carrots etc into spaghetti-like lengths?

10 Based on sales, which company is Britain's leading bread-maker?

ANSWERS 16

1 PAD THAI
2 HARRY POTTER
3 KELIS
4 SILVER SERVICE
5 JOANNE HARRIS
6 PICNIC BASKETS
7 GOLD BLEND
8 TITANIC BREWERY
9 SPIRALIZER
10 WARBURTON'S

QUIZ 17

1 Complete the title of the 1927 song *I Scream, You Scream, We all Scream for …*?

2 In which 1989 film did the director Rob Reiner's mother, sitting at a table near the two main characters in Katz's Deli in New York City, say "I'll have what she's having"?

3 In 1980 which retailer was the first in Britain to sell pre-packaged sandwiches – and they now sell over 1·5 million every week – that's approximately 1 in 5 of all bought sandwiches?

4 What name for a meal of cheese and bread served with pickle and salad, was coined by the English Country Cheese Council in the early 1970s?

5 Which character in a 1991 film said: "A census-taker once tried to test me. I ate his liver with some fava beans and a nice Chianti"?

6 Which biscuit is nicknamed a squashed fly biscuit?

7 In his 1970 hit *Nothing Rhymed* who sang: "When I'm drinking my Bonaparte shandy, eating more than enough apple pies. Will I glance at my screen and see real human beings starve right to death in front of my eyes?"?

8 Which company brews Hop House 13, a double-hopped lager made with Irish barley?

9 Which breed of dog is often depicted with a brandy barrel its around neck?

10 Which dish is made from chopped raw beef formed as a patty and served with onion, capers and a raw egg yolk on top?

ANSWERS 17

1 ICE CREAM
2 WHEN HARRY MET SALLY
3 MARKS & SPENCER
4 PLOUGHMAN'S LUNCH
5 HANNIBAL LECTER
6 GARIBALDI
7 GILBERT O'SULLIVAN
8 GUINNESS
9 ST. BERNARD
10 STEAK TARTARE

QUIZ 18

1 Cadbury says of which of its chocolate bars, that was launched in 1958, "You can still find its nobbly goodness in shops today"?

2 The fate of the father of which rabbit was to be put into a pie, after he had ventured into Mrs. McGregor's garden and had "an accident there"

3 Founded in France in 1765 by an Irishman, the Hennessy company is the world's leading producer of what drink?

4 Which Leonardo da Vinci mural painting covers the back wall of the dining room of the Santa Maria delle Grazie church in Milan?

5 Philip J. Fry, a pizza delivery boy who was frozen for 1,000 years, is the main character in which animated TV series?

6 Which drink was once sold in part-dimpled glass bottles and wrapped in yellow cellophane?

7 Which 1993 comedy 'Scottish' film character told her 'employer' that her husband was fond of a drink and it was drink that killed him? He was hit by a Guinness truck!

8 With a name that means 'fragrant' what is the best-selling variety of rice bought in the UK?

9 Opal Fruits became Starburst, what did Opal Mints become?

10 Which vegetable might you cooked Duchesse style?

ANSWERS 18

1 PICNIC
2 PETER RABBIT
3 COGNAC
4 THE LAST SUPPER
5 FUTURAMA
6 LUCOZADE
7 MRS. DOUBTFIRE
8 BASMATI
9 PACERS
10 POTATOES

QUIZ 19

1 According to the British Egg Information Service how many million eggs a day are eaten in the UK: 8 million, 16 million or 32 million?

2 Which fruit squash brand has been a fixture of tennis's Wimbledon fortnight since 1935 where the bottles can be seen on the umpires' chairs?

3 In 2000 which Conservative politician claimed that he downed up to 14 pints of beer a day as a teenager when working on a holiday job delivering to pubs and clubs?

4 In which London building is the Terrace Caféteria, Strangers' Dining Room, Churchill Grill Room and Bellamy's Self-Service Restaurant among other other eateries, lounges and bars?

5 What are the two main ingredients of an Aloo Gobi Indian dish?

6 Which US food brand's logo is an elderly African-American man with a bow tie and said to have been based on a Chicago maître d' named Frank Brown but this story is unverified?

7 In which country did fondue-style cooking originate?

8 What is the name of the ice cream dessert range at McDonald's restaurants that incorporate other brand name confections? E.g. Galaxy Ripple?

9 In Chinese cuisine what meat is used in a Char Siu dish?

10 Which song character, a 52 year-old delivery man, was killed after being struck underneath his heart by a rock cake thrown by Two Ton Ted From Teddington and was then caught in the eye by a stale pork pie?

ANSWERS 19

1 32 MILLION
2 ROBINSON'S
3 WILLIAM HAGUE
4 HOUSE OF COMMONS (PARLIAMENT)
5 POTATO & CAULIFLOWER
6 UNCLE BEN'S
7 SWITZERLAND
8 McFLURRY
9 PORK
10 ERNIE THE FASTEST MILKMAN IN THE WEST

QUIZ 20

1 Which 1974 film featured a night time meal of beans that brought on a famous farting session around the campfire?

2 Italian White and French Black are the two most highly prized varieties of which fungi?

3 Which cartoon character's original boyfriend, indeed one time fiancée, was a character called Harold Hamgravy but usually just known as Ham Gravy?

4 Second man on the moon Buzz Aldrin appeared in a TV advert for what brand name breakfast food?

5 The cocktail consisting of 1 part Baileys and 1 part Sambuca is called a Slippery … what?

6 One of which American city's nicknames is Beantown?

7 What is the collective name for TV cooks Dave Myers and Simon 'Si' King?

8 What shape is the type of pasta called stelline?

9 Which brand is described by the makers thus: "Our sticky little loaves remain the UK's favourite malt loaf, made to a top secret recipe (it) is still loved by the nation. The secret's in the squidge."?

10 He's eaten everything from insects to raw snake and moose heart, but who said the worst thing he's eaten was semen-filled goat testicles which he did on a TV programme?

ANSWERS 20

1 BLAZING SADDLES
2 TRUFFLE
3 OLIVE OYL
4 QUAKER OATS
5 NIPPLE
6 BOSTON (Massachusetts)
7 THE HAIRY BIKERS
8 STAR-SHAPED
9 SOREEN
10 BEAR GRYLLS

QUIZ 21

1 According to the saying what can't you make without breaking eggs?

2 During World War 1 what simple meal came to be nicknamed Zepps (Zeppelins) in a cloud?

3 In which song does Bob Marley sing: "And then Georgie would make the fire lights, as it was logwood burnin' through the nights. Then we would cook cornmeal porridge, of which I'll share with you."?

4 In November 2013 which Jamaican athlete revealed that during his ten days in Beijing for the 2008 Olympics he ate an estimated 1,000 Chicken McNuggets?

5 In which 2008 animated comedy film do the two main characters run a "Dough to Door" bakery business called Top Bun?

6 Shrimp is another name for a prawn: true or false?

7 In 2004 which food brand dropped its albatross logo which it had been using since the 1930s?

8 Mansize Buttons is a product in the range of which Nestle chocolate brand?

9 In a restaurant kitchen the head cook is the chef (chef de cuisine in full) what is the second in command (or under chef) called?

10 These are the 'cooking' instructions for what: 1) Rip off lid. Whip out the sachet. Add boiling water to fill level. Leave alone for two minutes. 2) Stir. Leave alone for 2 minutes. 3) Stir again. Find sachet. Add contents. 4) Grab fork and dig in.

ANSWERS 21

1 OMELETTE
2 SAUSAGES & MASH
3 NO WOMAN, NO CRY
4 USAIN BOLT
5 A MATTER OF LOAF AND DEATH (Wallace & Gromit)
6 FALSE
7 BIRDSEYE
8 YORKIE
9 SOUS CHEF
10 POT NOODLE

QUIZ 22

1 Which beer brand's logo is a monocled huntsman holding a pint glass? (It had been dropped in 2000 but restored in 2010 in a more stylised form)

2 According to the Office for National Statistics what was the average price of an 800g sliced white loaf of bread in December 2016?

3 In the year after the release of which 1995 film did sales of pork decrease by 10% in the USA?

4 Which sauce is the traditional accompaniment to roast pork?

5 In which 1960s American TV sitcom did Lily used to say to her son Eddie: "Don't just sit there, wolf down your food." which would, for example, have been rolled hyena-foot roast, cream of vulture soup, fillet of dragon and chopped lizard livers?

6 Which Scottish brewing company used to have pictures of women, their so-called 'Lager Lovelies', on their cans between 1969 and 1991?

7 Which French company, whose name means 'the crucible', is known for its colourful enamelled cast-iron cookware?

8 "Someone left a cake out in the rain" is a line from which song?

9 As in Edward Lear's nonsense poem what foodstuff did The Owl and The Pussycat take to sea with them in a beautiful pea green boat?

10 Running for 3 series between 1999 and 2001 what was the title of Jamie Oliver's first TV series?

ANSWERS 22

1 TETLEY
2 £1·01
3 BABE
4 APPLE SAUCE
5 THE MUNSTERS
6 TENNENT'S
7 LE CREUSET
8 MacARTHUR PARK
9 HONEY
10 THE NAKED CHEF

QUIZ 23

1 What would you drink from glasses whose shapes are called Conique, Tulip and Nonic?

2 What dessert is used in Cockney rhyming slang to mean 'sweetheart'?

3 What butter brand did former Sex Pistols singer John Lydon advertise on TV saying "It's not about Great Britain. It's about great butter!"?

4 What word can come before tea, cheese, bun and puff?

5 What type of food is Cornish Yarg?

6 Jack Daniel's whiskey cannot be bought in Lynchburg, Tennessee, the town that is home to the Jack Daniel's distillery: true or false?

7 Complete the proverb: "Breakfast like a king, lunch like a prince, dine (or sup) like a ..."?

8 Drumhead is a variety of which vegetable?

9 Hawaiians are the world's biggest consumers per capita of what brand name canned meat-based product?

10 How many flavours of Rowntree's Fruit Gums are there?

ANSWERS 23

1 BEER
2 TREACLE TART
3 COUNTRY LIFE
4 CREAM
5 CHEESE
6 TRUE (Lynchburg is in Moore County - a 'dry' county)
7 PAUPER
8 CABBAGE
9 SPAM
10 FIVE

QUIZ 24

1 Lyrics from which song? "Now when you pick a pawpaw or a prickly pear. And you prick a raw paw, next time beware. Don't pick the prickly pear by the paw. When you pick a pear try to use the claw. But you don't need to use the claw when you pick a pear of the big pawpaw"?

2 People of which North West England town are (usually pejoratively) nicknamed Pie-eaters?

3 Which sauce is a speciality of chicken dishes in Nando's restaurants?

4 Which US TV series had episodes called 'The One With the Cake', 'The One With the Dozen Lasagnes' and 'The One With the Cheesecakes', among others?

5 In 2000 what did footballer Roy Keane call people who attend football matches for the luxury corporate hospitality boxes and not for actually supporting the team?

6 In Act 2 of which ballet do Clara and the Prince travel to the Land of Sweets which is run by the Sugar Plum Fairy?

7 Wavy Gravy (Hugh Nanton Romney) was the MC at which 1969 music festival who one day said to the crowd: "Good morning. What we have in mind is breakfast in bed for 400,000 people"?

8 What was Heinz's first canned soup?

9 What, at one time, was advertised with the slogan "Lip-smackin', thirst-quenchin', ace-tastin', motivatin', good-buzzin', cool-talkin', high-walkin', fast-livin', ever-givin', cool-fizzin'"?

10 Which singer's long-time cook was Mary Jenkins Langston who created his favourite snack – a fried peanut butter and banana sandwich?

ANSWERS 24

1 THE BEAR NECESSITIES
2 WIGAN
3 PERI PERI
4 FRIENDS
5 PRAWN SANDWICH BRIGADE
6 THE NUTCRACKER
7 WOODSTOCK
8 CREAM OF TOMATO
9 PEPSI (Originally Pepsi Cola)
10 ELVIS PRESLEY

QUIZ 25

1 In the lyrics of Don McLean's song *American Pie* "them good old boys were drinking ..." what?

2 How many units of alcohol are there in one 70cl bottle of wine with alcohol by volume strength of 13%?

3 Which rich fruit cake decorated with split almonds was named after a city in eastern Scotland?

4 Who attended the 2010 MTV Video Music Awards in Los Angeles in a dress made of raw meat?

5 In which 1979 film does Graham Chapman, as a food vendor at a gladiatorial event, call out his wares; "Larks' tongues. Wrens' livers. Chaffinch brains. Jaguars' earlobes. Wolf nipple chips. Get 'em while they're hot. They're lovely."?

6 In which US western TV series from 1959 to 1973 was Hop Sing the Chinese cook at the Ponderosa Ranch?

7 At the summit of which Welsh pass is the Ponderosa Café?

8 What is the name of the small basket that strawberries and other soft fruits are sold or served in?

9 What is the maximum number of Michelin stars a restaurant can be awarded?

10 What is traditionally grated on top of an egg custard tart?

ANSWERS 25

1 WHISKEY AND RYE
2 9 UNITS
3 DUNDEE CAKE
4 LADY GAGA
5 MONTY PYTHON'S LIFE OF BRIAN
6 BONANZA
7 HORSESHOE PASS (Welsh: Bwlch yr Oernant)
8 PUNNET
9 3 STARS
10 NUTMEG

QUIZ 26

1 In 1990 which film star, with others, opened the Tribeca Grill at 375 Greenwich Street, Manhattan in New York?

2 What is the official sports energy drink of the Football Association?

3 What name is given to a drink consisting of champagne and Guinness?

4 What is the common name for the fleshy protuberance visible at the posterior end of a cooked chicken?

5 Which vegetable's scientific name is *Allium porrum*?

6 What used to be advertised with the slogan "Graded grains make finer flour"?

7 Which British cheese is traditionally accompanied by a glass of port?

8 Once voted the greatest ever TV comedy one-liner, what was Peter Kay as Brian Potter in *Phoenix Nights* referring to when he said "It's the future. I've tasted it."?

9 In which 1992 film does Harvey Keitel say to Tim Roth: "I'm hungry. Let's get a taco"?

10 Which came first: the two or four finger Kit-Kat?

ANSWERS 26

1 ROBERT DE NIRO

2 LUCOZADE SPORT

3 BLACK VELVET

4 PARSON'S NOSE (aka Pope's or Sultan's Nose)

5 LEEK

6 HOMEPRIDE

7 STILTON

8 GARLIC BREAD

9 RESERVOIR DOGS

10 FOUR FINGER

QUIZ 27

1 Which company's slogan is "Better ingredients. Better pizza"?

2 In what region of the UK might you cook or reheat your food in a popty ping?

3 What food in Aussie slang is a snag?

4 In which European capital city is chef René Redzepi's two Michelin-starred and award-winning Noma restaurant?

5 In *Coronation Street* what is the name of the café-cum-snack bar on Victoria Street?

6 In which 2007 animated film is Peter O'Toole the voice of restaurant critic and writer Anton Ego?

7 As in the lyrics of The Beatles song *Lucy in the Sky with Diamonds* what do the rocking horse people eat at the bridge by the fountain?

8 Two nosey old ladies named Margaret and Mabel used to appear in TV adverts for which frozen food brand?

9 In 1937 which brand was the UK's first canned rice pudding?

10 Which village, a suburb of Trieste in Italy, gives its name to a popular sparkling wine?

ANSWERS 27

1 PAPA JOHN'S
2 WALES (Popty ping is a Welsh name given to microwave oven)
3 SAUSAGE
4 COPENHAGEN
5 ROY'S ROLLS
6 RATATOUILLE
7 MARSHMALLOW PIES
8 AUNT BESSIE'S
9 AMBROSIA
10 PROSECCO

QUIZ 28

1 In cockney rhyming slang what does 'pig's ear' mean?

2 What is the name of the building in London, previously called the Swiss Re building, and also nicknamed the Gherkin or Erotic Gherkin?

3 What name is given to the crisp residue of pork fat left after rendering lard?

4 Which KFC slogan was replaced by "Nobody does chicken like KFC"?

5 What is the base layer ingredient inside a Mars bar?

6 In The Netherlands what food is a saucijzebroodje?

7 Which whisky brand's logo is The Striding Man?

8 *The Restaurant At The End Of The Universe* is the second book in which series by Douglas Adams?

9 Complete the name of this dish from the menu in a 1970 *Monty Python's Flying Circus* sketch: "Lobster Thermidor aux crevettes with a Mornay sauce served in a Provençale manner with shallots and aubergines garnished with truffle pâté, brandy and with a fried egg on top and …"

10 What female name (but two slightly different spellings) is both a tomato and basil pizza and a tequila-based cocktail?

ANSWERS 28

1 BEER
2 30 ST. MARY AXE
3 SCRATCHINGS
4 FINGERLICKIN' GOOD
5 NOUGAT
6 SAUSAGE ROLL
7 JOHNNIE WALKER
8 THE HITCHHIKER'S GUIDE TO THE GALAXY
9 SPAM
10 MARGHERITA / MARGARITA

QUIZ 29

1 Which Japanese noodle restaurant chain was founded by Alan Yau in 1992 and whose name means 'naughty child' in Japanese?

2 In which North Yorkshire town are the Tower, John Smith's and Samuel Smith's breweries?

3 Which brand has the largest share of the UK ambient packaged cake market?

4 Which food writer and TV presenter was born in Bath on 24 March 1935 and won the award for Best TV judge at the National Television Awards in January 2017?

5 Which alcoholic drink is mixed with honey to make an Irish Mist cocktail

6 In Italian cuisine what is ragù?

7 Which singer-songwriter character, the creation of Sheffield native Graham Fellows, includes in his repertoire the songs *The Toaster Song*, *Red Wine and Hobnobs*, *One Cup of Tea is Never Enough (But 2 is 1 Too Many)* and *Two Margarines*?

8 In the opening sequence of which 1977 film is John Travolta seen strutting down the street eating two slices of pizza on top of each other?

9 Which mints were advertised as being "a minty bit stronger"?

10 What was the slogan used on Wall's ice cream tricycles when they introduced them in the 1920s? (And also on the vans that came later)

ANSWERS 29

1 WAGAMAMA
2 TADCASTER
3 MR. KIPLING
4 MARY BERRY
5 WHISKEY
6 A (MEAT-BASED) SAUCE
7 JOHN SHUTTLEWORTH
8 SATURDAY NIGHT FEVER
9 TREBOR MINTS
10 STOP ME AND BUY ONE

QUIZ 30

1 In which film do two dogs share a plate of spaghetti and meatballs while restaurateur Tony serenades them on the accordion with the song *Bella Notte*?

2 Little Gem is a variety of what?

3 What flavour is the filling in a Bounty bar?

4 In which US sitcom (and earlier film) set in Korea in the 1950s is there a drinking establishment called Rosie's Bar?

5 In the Happy Families card game what is Mr. Bun's occupation?

6 Which 1984 No.1 single begins: "No New Year's Day to celebrate. No chocolate-covered candy hearts to give away."?

7 One of which French President's nicknames was La Grande Asperge (The Big Asparagus)?

8 Which grape is used to make Chablis wine?

9 What ingredient gives a Nestlé Crunch (originally Dairy Crunch) its crunch?

10 What does IPA stand for as in an IPA beer?

ANSWERS 30

1 LADY AND THE TRAMP
2 LETTUCE
3 COCONUT
4 M*A*S*H
5 BAKER
6 I JUST CALLED TO SAY I LOVE YOU (Stevie Wonder)
7 CHARLES DE GAULLE
8 CHARDONNAY
9 CRISPED RICE
10 INDIA PALE ALE

QUIZ 31

1 Which Italian confectionery company uses approximately 25% of the all world's hazelnut production?

2 Apart from music what links the bands Motörhead, Iron Maiden, Super Furry Animals, Elbow, and Status Quo?

3 Who did chef and restaurateur Marco Pierre White once call "a fat chef with a drum kit"?

4 Which character in a 1953 novel, the first of a series, says to a barman: "Three measures of Gordon's, one of vodka, half a measure of Kina Lillet. Shake it very well until it's ice cold, then add a thin slice of lemon peel. Got it?"?

5 Which yoghurt brand was promoted as "The full of fitness food"?

6 Which English king was noted for opulent 14 course banquets at Hampton Court Palace where some of the dishes would typically be grilled beaver tails, spit-roasted boar and roasted swan all made by around 200 kitchen staff?

7 On 8 January 1940 food rationing began in Britain. What were the first three foods to be rationed?

8 What is the name of the so-called hangover cure consisting of a raw egg in tomato juice, wine vinegar, pepper and Worcestershire sauce? (Although ingredients can vary)

9 In 1989 Bill Wyman opened a London restaurant called Sticky Fingers, named after an album by which band of which he was a member?

10 Which Morland brewery beer, whose mascot is a fox, was first brewed in 1979 to commemorate the 50th anniversary of the MG car factory opening in Abingdon?

ANSWERS 31

1 FERRERO
2 ALL HAVE (OR HAVE HAD) THEIR OWN BEERS BREWED
3 JAMIE OLIVER
4 JAMES BOND
5 SKI
6 HENRY VIII
7 BACON, BUTTER AND SUGAR
8 PRAIRIE OYSTER
9 THE ROLLING STONES
10 OLD SPECKLED HEN

QUIZ 32

1 What is the name of the chocolate egg made by Ferrero that contains a children's toy inside a plastic shell?

2 What was advertised on TV by a drumming gorilla playing along to the song *In The Air Tonight* by Phil Collins?

3 On which animated character's shelves can be found the books *Brighton Roquefort*, *Brie Encounter*, *East of Edam*, *Grated Expectations*, *Fromage to Eternity*, *Swiss Cheese Family Robinson* and other similarly cheesy-titled tomes?

4 In which country are Jacob's Creek wines made?

5 What is the name of the 15% ABV fortified, high caffeine content wine made by Benedictine monks in Devon, the drinking of which in the past has been cited by some to be a major cause of crime, anti-social behaviour and social deprivation in Scotland?

6 What flavour soup is nicknamed Jewish Penicillin?

7 What is the most popular day of the week for eating fish and chips?

8 What type of food is a madeleine?

9 What does the Heinz company say exits the bottle unaided at 0.028 mph?

10 In which song are the lyrics: "From the park you hear the happy sound of a carousel. Mmmm. You can almost taste the hotdogs and French fries they sell".?

ANSWERS 32

1 KINDER SURPRISE
2 CADBURY DAIRY MILK
3 WALLACE (Of Wallace & Gromit)
4 AUSTRALIA
5 BUCKFAST
6 CHICKEN
7 FRIDAY
8 A CAKE
9 TOMATO KETCHUP
10 UNDER THE BOARDWALK

QUIZ 33

1 Which city was named Curry Capital of Britain in 2016 for the 6th year in a row?

2 Where can you buy a Big Daddy box meal containing The Daddy Burger, 1 piece of Original Recipe Chicken, large fries, regular side and a large drink?

3 Which BBC1 sitcom, that ran from 1982 to 1992, had a number of episodes where sausages appeared to be of significance to the storyline including 'The Sausage in the Wardrobe', The Sausages in the Trousers', 'Soup and Sausage' and 'The Nicked Knockwurst'?

4 Much of which classic 1942 film is set at a "gin joint" called Rick's Café Americain?

5 Who are the parents of toy characters Spud and Yam?

6 Who founded the General Seafood Corporation in 1920s America?

7 Complete the saying "You can't sip soup with a ..."?

8 In the West Country what name is given to rough, strong, dry cider?

9 In *Alice's Adventures In Wonderland* who is accused of stealing the tarts?

10 What word can come before bread, rice, sauce and sugar?

ANSWERS 33

1 BRADFORD
2 KFC
3 ALLO ALLO
4 CASABLANCA
5 MR. & MRS. POTATO HEAD
6 CLARENCE BIRDSEYE
7 KNIFE
8 SCRUMPY
9 THE KNAVE OF HEARTS
10 BROWN

QUIZ 34

1 What can be bought in Italy at a gelataria?

2 Born in Wallasey in 1966 who, in an earlier period of his career, was once head baker at the Dorchester, Chester Grosvenor & Spa and Cliveden hotels?

3 What is most commonly served, either on a stick or not, as the garnish in a Martini?

4 Which member of the Royal Family is president of the restaurant organisation the Scotch Beef Club?

5 Which Greyfriars' schoolboy glutton was created by writer Frank Richards?

6 In which 1989 film does Jack Nicholson say: "Never rub another man's rhubarb."?

7 Which singer and actor included the song *My Little Stick of Blackpool Rock* in his performance repertoire?

8 In which country did chutney's originate?

9 What is the name of The Krusty Krab's rival fast food place in *Spongebob Squarepants*?

10 What would you drink from a snifter glass?

ANSWERS 34

1 ICE CREAM
2 PAUL HOLLYWOOD
3 OLIVE
4 THE PRINCESS ROYAL (ANNE)
5 BILLY BUNTER
6 BATMAN
7 GEORGE FORMBY
8 INDIA
9 THE CHUM BUCKET
10 BRANDY

QUIZ 35

1 What activity would you be doing if you were chanting "Salt, mustard, vinegar, pepper. French almond rock. Bread and butter for our supper. That's all mother's got"?

2 Furenchi furai (フレンチフライ) is Japanese for what food?

3 What does a crêpe become if it comes with an orange and Grand Marnier sauce which is flambéed?

4 Which American realist painted *Chop Suey*, a 1929 picture of two women in conversation in a restaurant?

5 What is the flavour of the Mexican liqueur Kahlúa?

6 Pure Indulgence is a brand of which Dutch coffee company?

7 Which actor's time as the Doctor in *Doctor Who* was partial to Jelly Babies; a bag of which he always had with him?

8 According to tradition the top tier of a wedding cake is retained for what event?

9 The lyrics of which song begin: "When the moon hits your eye like a big pizza pie"?

10 Which character, voiced by Conrad Vernon in the *Shrek* films, was tortured by King Farquaad's bodyguard by having his legs cut off and dunked in a glass of milk?

ANSWERS 35

1 SKIPPING
2 FRENCH FRIES
3 CRÊPE SUZETTE
4 EDWARD HOPPER
5 COFFEE
6 DOUWE EGBERTS
7 TOM BAKER
8 FIRST ANNIVERSARY or CHRISTENING OF FIRST CHILD
9 THAT'S AMORE
10 GINGERBREAD MAN (GINGY)

QUIZ 36

1 Who wrote *The Princess and the Pea*?

2 Which TV and film character requests his beverage from the replicator by saying: "Tea. Earl Grey. Hot"?

3 Which boxer launched his Lean Mean Fat-Reducing Grilling Machine in 1994? (It wasn't invented by him but it's his name on it.)

4 The end credits of which cartoon series sees two families and two pets leave a drive-in movie in a car and go to Bronto Burgers & Ribs?

5 In which film does Jim Carrey perform the parting of the tomato soup?

6 In the 1970s and 1980s what was advertised by Ian Botham, Brian Clough and Peter Shilton – all of whom were unable to eat three?

7 By what name was Carling lager previously known, having dropped the name in 1997?

8 What is Burger King's signature sandwich?

9 Which dish on an Indian restaurant menu has a name which translates as 'two onions'?

10 Which American entertainer known for his dislike of children and dogs once said: "I cook with wine, sometimes I even add it to the food"?

ANSWERS 36

1 HANS CHRISTIAN ANDERSEN
2 CAPTAIN JEAN-LUC PICARD (Of the *Star Trek* franchise)
3 GEORGE FOREMAN
4 THE FLINTSTONES
5 BRUCE ALMIGHTY
6 SHREDDED WHEAT
7 CARLING BLACK LABEL
8 WHOPPER
9 DOPIAZA
10 W.C.FIELDS

QUIZ 37

1 What was the name of TV cook Fanny Cradock's husband who used to appear with her in TV programmes?

2 What is Garfield's favourite food?

3 Which Indiana Jones film features a dinner that includes chilled monkey brains and eyeball soup?

4 What is obtained from the dried swim bladders of fish and used for fining some beers and wines?

5 In 1988 which MP resigned from her position as a junior Health Minister over the salmonella in eggs controversy?

6 In an interview with Jonathan Ross in 2003 Madonna revealed that which beer, brewed by the Timothy Taylor brewery, was her favourite beer?

7 Which English stadium has 34 bars, 98 kitchens and 688 food and drink service points?

8 In the Royal Navy what name was given to the watered-down rum?

9 In which Lake District village is Sarah Nelson's gingerbread shop?

10 Which confections are called wienerbrød (Vienna bread) in Denmark?

ANSWERS 37

1 JOHNNY

2 LASAGNE

3 INDIANA JONES AND THE TEMPLE OF DOOM

4 ISINGLASS

5 EDWINA CURRIE

6 LANDLORD

7 WEMBLEY

8 GROG

9 GRASMERE

10 DANISH PASTRIES

QUIZ 38

1 In one *Fawlty Towers* episode an American by the name of Mr. Hamilton wanted what as his starter course but Basil said they were out of them?

2 What was advertised by Monkey and Al (played by Johnny Vegas before he was dropped)? (They had previously advertised ITV Digital)

3 Which 2009 animated film features wannabe scientist Flint Lockwood who invents the Diatonic Super Mutating Dynamic Food Replicator?

4 Which British eatery chain has Fat Charlie as the mascot? (Not necessarily seen on the outside of the restaurants anymore which are down to just 71 locations)

5 *Custard Pie* was the opening track on which group's sixth studio album *Physical Graffiti*?

6 Whose mint balls are made by William Santus & Co. of Wigan?

7 The final scene of which 1990 film sees Cher, Christina Ricci and Winona Ryder dancing to the song *If You Wanna Be Happy* while preparing food in a kitchen?

8 On which TV show do some of the participants undergo Bush Tucker challenges?

9 What is the world's best-selling brand of gin?

10 Kabanos is a Polish variety of what?

ANSWERS 38

1 WALDORF SALAD
2 PG TIPS
3 CLOUDY WITH A CHANCE OF MEATBALLS
4 LITTLE CHEF
5 LED ZEPPELIN
6 UNCLE JOE'S MINT BALLS
7 MERMAIDS
8 I'M A CELEBRITY … GET ME OUT OF HERE
9 GORDON'S
10 SAUSAGE

QUIZ 39

1 What type of pastry is used in making the Greek dish baklava?

2 In Sweden what food is called köttbullar which are traditionally served with boiled or mashed potatoes, lingonberry jam and gravy?

3 In which 1990 film does Julia Roberts send a snail flying across a posh restaurant which is caught by a waiter and she then says to the other people at the table "Slippery little suckers"?

4 Complete the proverb "Beer and wine and you'll feel fine. Wine and beer and you'll feel …"?

5 In which country's cuisine is jerk chicken a popular dish?

6 What brand of beer is Pedigree?

7 From what language are the words beef, courgette, omelette, salad, juice and bacon directly derived?

8 In which country is Gruyère (aka Greyerzer) cheese made?

9 What do we call what Americans call a bouillon cube?

10 What is the more common name for Chinese parsley?

ANSWERS 39

1 FILO
2 MEATBALLS
3 PRETTY WOMAN
4 QUEER
5 JAMAICA
6 MARSTON'S
7 FRENCH
8 SWITZERLAND
9 STOCK CUBE
10 CORIANDER

QUIZ 40

1 What is the name of the long, thin breadsticks usually eaten as appetizers in Italian restaurants?

2 What is the name of the restaurant in London, owned by Ruth Rogers, where the likes of Theo Randall, Jamie Oliver and Hugh Fearnley-Whittingstall trained?

3 Which Samoan-born chef has been a judge on the TV show *Masterchef: The Professionals* since 2009?

4 Teriyaki is a style of cooking in which country's cuisine?

5 Which American state capital is nicknamed The Big Pineapple?

6 Tenderstem is a variety of what green vegetable?

7 Which British Prime Minister was a huge fan of Pol Roger champagne?

8 On which train are the Côte d'Azur and Etoile du Nord restaurant cars?

9 What is the national fruit of India?

10 Which group had a 1988/89 hit single titled *Orange Crush*?

ANSWERS 40

1 GRISSINI
2 RIVER CAFÉ
3 MONICA GALETTI
4 JAPAN
5 HONOLULU
6 BROCCOLI
7 WINSTON CHURCHILL
8 VENICE-SIMPLON-ORIENT EXPRESS
9 MANGO
10 R.E.M.

QUIZ 41

1 What is the world's most expensive spice?

2 Leffe Blonde, Leffe Brune, Leffe Ruby and Leffe Nectar are brands of what drink?

3 Bombay Bad Boy is a flavour of what snack food brand?

4 Which sweets used to be advertised with the slogan "Wot a lot I got"?

5 What was the first name of Mr. Guinness who founded the brewery in Dublin in 1759?

6 On Friday 27 March 1998 who made her first ever visit to a pub; The Bridge Inn at Topsham near Exeter?

7 What is the name of the vegetarian equivalent of a shepherd's or cottage pie that uses adzuki beans and a grain (e.g. buckwheat) as substitute for the meat?

8 What do the letters BBE on food packaging stand for?

9 Chiquito is a chain of restaurants selling what type of food?

10 In which decade were oven chips launched in the UK?

ANSWERS 41

1 SAFFRON
2 BEER
3 POT NOODLE
4 SMARTIES
5 ARTHUR
6 QUEEN ELIZABETH II
7 RED DRAGON PIE
8 BEST BEFORE END
9 MEXICAN / TEX MEX
10 1970s (1979)

QUIZ 42

1 Which Nestlé chocolate used to be advertised with the slogan "Irresistabubble"? (A term coined by former advertising copywriter Salman Rushdie)

2 The chorus of which No.2 song from 2003 is: "A Pizza Hut, A Pizza Hut, Kentucky Fried Chicken and a Pizza Hut. A Pizza Hut, A Pizza Hut, Kentucky Fried Chicken and a Pizza Hut. McDonald's McDonald's, Kentucky Fried Chicken and a Pizza Hut. McDonald's McDonald's, Kentucky Fried Chicken and a Pizza Hut."

3 Which *South Park* character has a KFC addiction?

4 Which variety of potato is also the name of a potato crisps company founded in Edinburgh in 1947?

5 What grain is used in making a Scottish single malt whisky?

6 Which TV cook and writer has been dubbed "The Queen of Food Porn"?

7 Which wine is released in France on the third Thursday of November every year?

8 Which dessert's name is French and means 'burnt cream'?

9 How many units of alcohol are there in 4 pints of 4·4% ABV beer?

10 In 1954 French engineer Marc Grégoire invented the first of what type of saucepan?

ANSWERS 42

1 AERO

2 THE FAST FOOD SONG (By Fast Food Rockers)

3 ERIC CARTMAN

4 GOLDEN WONDER

5 BARLEY

6 NIGELLA LAWSON

7 BEAUJOLAIS NOUVEAU

8 CRÈME BRÛLÉE

9 10 UNITS

10 NON-STICK (TEFLON)

QUIZ 43

1 Which island in the British Isles has been dubbed The Land Of Kippers?

2 In France what is called boudin noir?

3 In Cockney rhyming slang what does Jacob's Crackers mean?

4 What is a Bloody Mary drink called without the vodka?

5 In 1994 which singer had a No.4 hit single with the song *Cornflake Girl*?

6 How many holes are there in a round Rich Tea biscuit?

7 Which egg product does the department store Fortnum & Mason in London claim to have invented in 1738?

8 A bottle of which brand of whiskey is in Frank Sinatra's coffin?

9 What is the name of the range of Walker's crisps that includes the flavours Mexican Fiery Sweet Chipotle, Thai Sweet Chilli, Caramelised Onion & Balsamic Vinegar, Roasted Chicken & Thyme, Vintage Cheddar and Onion Chutney, Gently Infused Lime with Thai Spices and Moroccan Spices with Sweet Tomato?

10 What is the name of the Greek and Turkish dish made from vine leaves stuffed with meat and rice?

ANSWERS 43

1 ISLE OF MAN
2 BLACK PUDDING / BLOOD SAUSAGE
3 KNACKERS
4 VIRGIN MARY
5 TORI AMOS
6 22
7 SCOTCH EGG
8 JACK DANIEL'S
9 SENSATIONS
10 DOLMADES / DOLMA

QUIZ 44

1 In which 1995 film was John Doe's first murder victim force-fed spaghetti until his stomach burst?

2 What drink is mixed with lager to make a Snakebite?

3 In Indian cuisine what are roti, paratha and puri?

4 In table setting etiquette is the dessert spoon placed above or below the dessert fork?

5 VAT 69 is a brand of what drink?

6 Which brand name soft drink did the Coca Cola bottling company in Germany create during World War II because they couldn't get Coca Cola syrup?

7 What is the American word for 'minced' beef?

8 In which Jack Kerouac novel does Sal Paradise say: "I ate another apple pie and ice cream; that's practically all the way across the country, I knew it was nutritious."?

9 Which brand of dairy products was named so by a Mr. Barrett, a director of a cheese-making firm, who dreamt up a story of a monk who lived by the River Yeo in Somerset?

10 According to the British Egg Information Service how for many minutes should a large egg be boiled for a completely set white and soft yolk?

ANSWERS 44

1 SEVEN (Styled as *'Se7en'*)
2 CIDER
3 BREADS
4 ABOVE
5 WHISKY
6 FANTA
7 GROUND BEEF
8 ON THE ROAD
9 ST. IVEL
10 3 MINUTES

QUIZ 45

1 What colour is a Granny Smith apple?

2 In which film does John Lennon, on finding a season ticket in his soup, say: "Oh I like a lot of seasoning in my soup"?

3 What term is used for a steak cooked rarer than rare?

4 In the song *How d'ya Like your Eggs in the Morning?* recorded by Dean Martin and Helen O'Connell, they like eggs with a kiss but with what do they like their toast?

5 What is known as the King of Spices?

6 In 1983 Lynda Bellingham became the mum in which family?

7 Which beer was advertised with the slogan "Refreshes the parts other beers cannot reach"?

8 In which comedy sketch TV show was there a sketch called 'Going for an English', a mickey-take of white British people who go for an 'Indian'?

9 Imports of what Scottish food have been banned in US by the Department of Agriculture since 1971? (Suggested the ban may be lifted in 2017)

10 Which coffee brand was named in the late 19th century by Joel Cheek after an hotel in Nashville, Tennessee?

ANSWERS 45

1 GREEN

2 HELP!

3 BLUE

4 A HUG

5 BLACK PEPPER

6 OXO FAMILY

7 HEINEKEN

8 GOODNESS GRACIOUS ME

9 HAGGIS

10 MAXWELL HOUSE

QUIZ 46

1 Which TV presenter was famously caught eating a Mars bar on TV when the camera unexpectedly went back to him in a 1987 BBC election night programme?

2 Starting in the 1960s what brand of bread was advertised on TV with people flying in hot air balloons and the song *I Can't Let Maggie Go* by Honeybus?

3 As in the title of the song, what is the name of the Spanish and French-influenced dish of Louisiana that The Carpenters sang about "on the bayou" in charts of 1973?

4 The most typical meal at which restaurant chain founded in 1955, and Britain's largest of its kind in the 1970s & 80s, was a sherry aperitif followed by prawn cocktail starter, steak and chips and Black Forest gateau for afters?

5 The song *The Candy Man Can*, performed by actor Aubrey Woods, is a song on the original soundtrack of which 1971 musical film?

6 In a poll by YouGov in 2014 it was revealed that most people think that the packaging colours for which two flavours of Walker's crisps are the wrong way round?

7 Which vodka brand was created by Lars Olsson Smith in Sweden in 1879?

8 Which filled puff pastry food's name is French and literally means 'flight in the wind'?

9 What type of quill-shaped pasta comes in smooth form called lisce and in ridged form called rigate?

10 Who wrote the 1945 book *The Way to Cook* and later in the decade became Britain's first celebrity TV chef?

ANSWERS 46

1 DAVID DIMBLEBY

2 NIMBLE

3 JAMBALAYA

4 BERNI INN

5 WILLY WONKA AND THE CHOCOLATE FACTORY

6 CHEESE & ONION and SALT & VINEGAR

7 ABSOLUT

8 VOL AU VENT

9 PENNE

10 PHILIP HARBEN

QUIZ 47

1 Brewed under license in the UK by Heineken, complete the name of the lager Kronenbourg ...?

2 What is the name of the aromatic Italian vinegar made from heated Trebbiano grape juice and aged for several years in wooden casks?

3 Which South Yorkshire town gave its name to a double loin chop cut from a saddle of lamb?

4 What does 'petit pois' mean in English?

5 Which company's logo is based on the O'Neill harp (aka the Brian Boru harp)?

6 Which animated character is very fond of ring donuts with pink icing and sprinkles?

7 In 1968/69 which 'preserve' group had their only UK No.1 single with *Ob-La-Di Ob-La-Da*?

8 What animal, scientific name *Cavia porcellus*, is a popular fried or roasted delicacy in Peru where the animal's name is cuy?

9 Which Hollywood star established a food company in 1982 starting with a salad dressing and developing into pasta sauces etc, the profits of which were given to charity?

10 Which characters appear in TV adverts for Warburton's giant crumpets?

ANSWERS 47

1 1664
2 BALSAMIC
3 BARNSLEY
4 LITTLE PEAS
5 GUINNESS
6 HOMER SIMPSON
7 MARMALADE
8 GUINEA PIG
9 PAUL NEWMAN
10 THE MUPPETS

QUIZ 48

1 In a sketch in *The Two Ronnies* TV show Ronnie Barker was a disgruntled waiter serving Ronnie Corbett and his wife in a restaurant but the only dishes on the menu contained what bird?

2 What were originally advertised with the slogan "Once you pop you can't stop"?

3 To what name did Sugar Puffs change in 2014?

4 Which drink's name is Spanish and means 'strained pineapple'?

5 Which singer, who had a No.1 single in 1955 with the song *Softly Softly*, has her name used in Cockney rhyming slang to mean 'curry'?

6 In Australia there is a dish called a pie floater. In what does the pie float?

7 It was announced on 3 February 2016 that Liverpool firefighter Patrick McBride had got the job as which revived TV advert character?

8 What does 'poivre' mean as in steak au poivre?

9 It has been reported, and seen on TV at least once, that which prominent person enjoys a daily pre-lunch gin and Dubonnet?

10 On what subject are the following people experts and / or writers: Jilly Goolden, Oz Clarke, Susie Barrie, Jancis Robinson, Olly Smith?

ANSWERS 48

1 ROOK
2 PRINGLES
3 HONEY MONSTER PUFFS
4 PIÑA COLADA
5 RUBY MURRAY
6 PEA SOUP
7 MILK TRAY MAN
8 PEPPER
9 QUEEN ELIZABETH II
10 WINE

QUIZ 49

1 Three of what letter of the alphabet were marked on jugs of Moonshine, illicitly-made liquor in the US, to indicate that it had gone through the required number of distillations?

2 What food was used as the working title of Paul McCartney's song *Yesterday*?

3 Which chocolate bar used to be advertised with the slogan "The sweet you can eat between meals"?

4 Complete the opening lines from the song *The Wild Rover*: "I've been a wild rover for many a year, and I spend all my money on ..."

5 In US diners and delis a classic pastrami sandwich would usually be made with what type of bread?

6 Which comedy act had a 1975 hit single called *Black Pudding Bertha (The Queen of Northern Soul)*?

7 What two colours is the sponge in a Battenberg cake?

8 Which BBC TV programme carried out an April Fool's joke in 1957 in an item about the spaghetti harvest in Switzerland?

9 Which American pop artist created a series of screen prints of Campbell's soup cans in the 1960s?

10 According to the company how many million Mars bars are made every day at their Slough factory?

ANSWERS 49

1 XXX
2 SCRAMBLED EGGS
3 MILKY WAY
4 WHISKEY AND BEER
5 RYE
6 THE GOODIES
7 YELLOW AND PINK
8 PANORAMA
9 ANDY WARHOL
10 3 MILLION

QUIZ 50

1 Introduced in 1912 what is the best-selling cookie brand in the USA?

2 In which old Saturday morning children's TV show was The Phantom Flan-Flinger?

3 What did Delia Smith make for the front cover photo of the 1969 *Let It Bleed* album by The Rolling Stones?

4 Which brand beer has been advertised on TV by movie star Jean-Claude van Damme making snow angels among other things?

5 Which TV advert family consists of Mama, Papa, Carlo, Sophia, Nick and Nina?

6 The comic book strip 'Bully Beef and Chips' first appeared in 1967 in which comic?

7 In which 2001 sequel film does Julianne Moore awaken to find Krendler seated at the table set for an elegant dinner. Weakened by the drugs, she looks on in horror as the title character removes part of Krendler's prefrontal cortex, sautés it, and feeds it to him?

8 Gaffer is the leader of which beverage brand's mascots – the others being Sydney, Maurice, Tina, Gordon, Clarence and Archie?

9 Which brand name drink is known as "Scotland's other national drink"?

10 What cheese is an ingredient of a Greek salad?

ANSWERS 50

1 OREO
2 TISWAS
3 THE CAKE
4 COORS LIGHT
5 DOLMIO
6 THE DANDY
7 HANNIBAL
8 TETLEY TEA FOLK
9 IRN BRU
10 FETA

I hope you enjoyed this book. There will be more coming, if indeed they are not already for sale on Amazon. Check them out and please review.

Printed in Great Britain
by Amazon